Lewis and Clark

Jennifer Strand

abdopublishing.com

Published by Abdo Zoom™, PO Box 398166, Minneapolis, Minnesota 55439. Copyright © 2017 by Abdo Consulting Group, Inc. International copyrights reserved in all countries. No part of this book may be reproduced in any form without written permission from the publisher. Abdo Zoom™ is a trademark and logo of Abdo Consulting Group, Inc.

Printed in the United States of America, North Mankato, Minnesota
072016
092016

Cover Photo: Everett Historical/Shutterstock Images, left, right
Interior Photos: Everett Historical/Shutterstock Images, 1 (left), 1 (right), 5, 9 (left), 9 (right); Andrew Fuller/Shutterstock Images, 4–5; North Wind Picture Archives, 6, 10, 10–11, 12, 15, 18–19; Shutterstock Images, 7; Kris Wiktor/Shutterstock Images, 8–9; iStockphoto, 13; Ira Block/National Geographic Creative, 14; Rabbit Hole Photo/iStockphoto, 16–17; Png Studio Photography/Shutterstock Images, 17

Editor: Emily Temple
Series Designer: Madeline Berger
Art Direction: Dorothy Toth

Publisher's Cataloging-in-Publication Data
Names: Strand, Jennifer, author.
Title: Lewis and Clark / by Jennifer Strand.
Description: Minneapolis, MN : Abdo Zoom, [2017] | Series: Pioneering
    explorers | Includes bibliographical references and index.
Identifiers: LCCN 2016941517 | ISBN 9781680792430 (lib. bdg.) |
    ISBN 9781680794113 (ebook) | 9781680795004 (Read-to-me ebook)
Subjects: LCSH: Lewis, Meriwether,1774-1809--Juvenile literature. | Clark,
    William, 1770-1838--Juvenile literature. | Explorers--West (U.S.)--
    Biography--Juvenile literature. | Lewis and Clark Expedition (1804-1806)--
    Juvenile literature.
Classification: DDC 917.804/2/0922 [B]--dc23
LC record available at http://lccn.loc.gov/2016941517

Table of Contents

Introduction

Meriwether Lewis and William Clark were explorers. The United States bought land west of the Mississippi River. Lewis and Clark explored it.

They traveled many miles.

Early Life

Meriwether and William grew up on **plantations**.

William later lived on the frontier. Meriwether liked to study plants and animals.

Leaders

Lewis and Clark joined the army.
That is where they met.

They learned how
to live in the wild.

Lewis worked for
President Thomas Jefferson.

Jefferson wanted to find a **waterway** to the Pacific Ocean. He asked Lewis and Clark to find one.

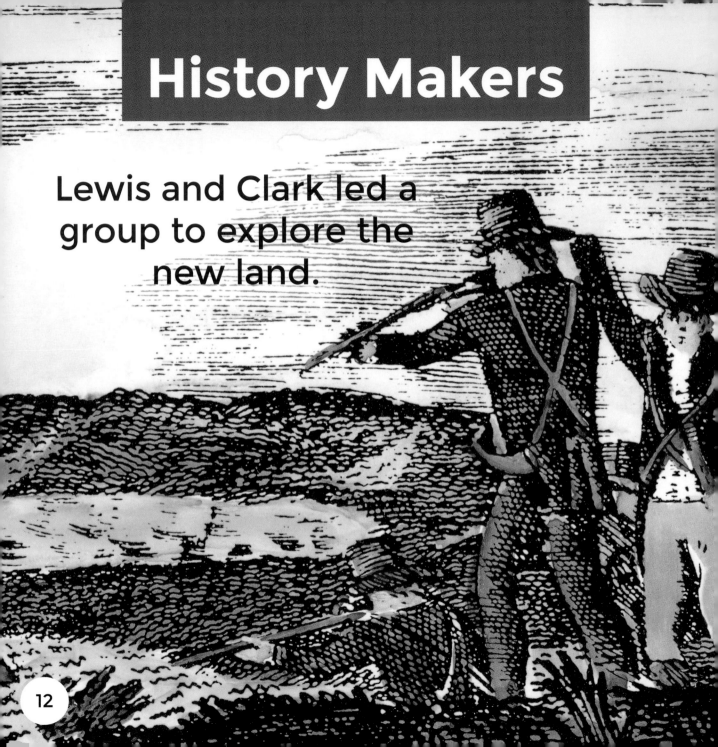

History Makers

Lewis and Clark led a group to explore the new land.

They traveled along
the Missouri River.

They made maps.
They wrote about what they found.

They also tried to keep peace with the Native Americans.

Legacy

Lewis and Clark went to the Pacific Ocean. Then they returned home.

They were greeted as heroes.

Lewis died in 1809. Clark died in 1838. Their notes helped pioneers live on the frontier. This helped the United States grow.

...green and common...

the

point ?

pine, being from 25 to 27 in ?

a deep green, their point

the extremity of the rib

not know the fruit or ?

bles a plant Common to

19

Quick Stats

Meriwether Lewis

Born: August 18, 1774

Birthplace: near Charlottesville, Virginia

Died: October 11, 1809

William Clark

Born: August 1, 1770

Birthplace: Caroline County, Virginia

Died: September 1, 1838

Known For: Lewis and Clark explored the western United States in the early 1800s.

Key Dates

1770: William Clark is born on August 1.

1774: Meriwether Lewis is born on August 18.

1804–1806: Lewis and Clark lead the Corps of Discovery. They explore the West.

1805: Lewis and Clark reach the Pacific Ocean.

1809: Lewis dies on October 11.

1838: Clark dies on September 1.

Glossary

explorer - a person who travels to new places.

frontier - land where few people live.

pioneer - a person who does something that few have done before.

plantation - a large farm where crops are grown to be sold.

waterway - a route for travel by water.

Booklinks

For more information
on Lewis and Clark, please visit
booklinks.abdopublishing.com

 Zoom In on Biographies!

Learn even more with the Abdo Zoom
Biographies database. Check out
abdozoom.com for more information.

Index